THE APOSTLES' CREED

The Apostles' Creed

A Faith to Live By

C. E. B. Cranfield

continuum

LONDON • NEW YORK

Continuum

The Tower Building
11 York Road
London SE1 7NX, UK

15 East 26th Street
New York 10010
USA

www.continuumbooks.com

First published 1993
Reprinted 1998
This edition 2004

ISBN 0 8264 7391 1

British Library Cataloguing-in-Publication Data
A catalogue record for this book is available from the British Library

Printed and bound in Great Britain by Cromwell Press, Trowbridge, Wiltshire

Contents

Preface

There are already many excellent expositions of the Apostles' Creed. But it seemed to me that there was room for a fresh exposition on the limited scale and of the sort attempted in the following pages. I have tried to explain the Creed, as I understand it, as briefly and straightforwardly as possible without being superficial.

I hope that hard-pressed pastors, who, along with many other urgent commitments, must prepare people for confirmation or church membership, may find this little book helpful, dealing as it does with a considerable amount of the ground that a confirmation class may be expected to cover or that prospective church members will need to know. (The importance of such classes for the church's health, can, I think, hardly be emphasized too much.)

But I also hope that many others will find this book useful, particularly those church members who feel a need for a more definite and coherent faith — both for the sake of their own continuing Christian life and also in order that they might be more ready and able to give an answer concerning the hope that is in them. I hope that it may also be of interest to some, who, while not being Christians themselves, are ready to give a little time to trying to discover what it is that Christians believe.

My very warm thanks are due to Dr. John W. Simpson, Jr. of Wm. B. Eerdmans Publishing Co. for his painstaking endeavors to improve my English style.

Durham, September 1992   C.E.B.C.

Preface to the third impression

The world in which we are living in the latter part of 2003 is much more dangerous than the world of 1993, when this book was first published. The opening years of the twenty-first century have already seen the destruction of the Twin Towers on 11 September 2001; the declaration, in response to it, of the so-called "war against terrorism", which has brought with it an erosion of civil rights; the war in Afghanistan; the calling in question of the inviolability of the Geneva Convention; the war launched against Iraq despite the strong objections of very many; and the serious weakening of the authority of the United Nations and of respect for international law. In such a world, with its continuing obscene inequalities between the rich nations and the poor, its flagrant injustices and hypocrisies, and its very understandable resentments and hatreds, the need for Christians to try very hard to think clearly and coherently both about the gospel and about the moral and political obligations which flow from it for those who believe, is surely becoming more and more urgent. My hope is that this third impression will encourage more Christians to do this.

Durham, June 2003   C.E.B.C.

THE APOSTLES' CREED

The traditional version of the Apostles' Creed

I believe in God the Father Almighty,
    maker of heaven and earth;
And in Jesus Christ his only Son our Lord;
    who was conceived by the Holy Ghost,
    born of the Virgin Mary,
    suffered under Pontius Pilate,
    was crucified, dead, and buried.
    He descended into hell.
    The third day he rose again from the dead.
    He ascended into heaven,
    and sitteth on the right hand of God
        the Father Almighty.
    From thence He shall come to judge the quick
        and the dead.
I believe in the Holy Ghost,
    the holy catholic Church,
    the communion of saints,
    the forgiveness of sins,
    the resurrection of the body,
    and the life everlasting.

A modern version of the Apostles' Creed

I believe in God, the Father almighty,
    creator of heaven and earth.

I believe in Jesus Christ, his only Son, our Lord.
    He was conceived by the power of the Holy Spirit
        and born of the Virgin Mary.
    He suffered under Pontius Pilate,
        was crucified, died, and was buried.
    He descended to the dead.
    On the third day he rose again.
    He ascended into heaven,
        and is seated at the right hand of the Father.
    He will come again to judge the living and the dead.

I believe in the Holy Spirit,
    the holy catholic Church,
    the communion of saints,
    the forgiveness of sins,
    the resurrection of the body,
    and the life everlasting.

This modern version of the Creed is from *Prayers We Have in Common*, which was produced by the International Consultation on English Texts and published in 1970.

The Origin and Importance of the Creed

The Apostles' Creed is true to its name in the sense that it is a compact and felicitous summary of New Testament teaching. It can be traced back in almost precisely its present form to the eighth century and with only slight variations as far back as the sixth.

The Old Roman Creed, an early statement of Christian beliefs used in connection with baptism, was quoted in Greek by Marcellus of Ancyra in A.D. 340 and in Latin by Rufinus about A.D. 400. It is found in Greek in question form in Hippolytus's *Apostolic Tradition* early in the third century, and Hippolytus's use of it probably implies that it existed in the latter part of the second century, when the Roman church still used Greek. This early creed is recognizably akin to our Apostles' Creed.

Apparently, the Roman Creed was elaborated a little in the church north of the Alps, and then, after the time of Charlemagne (who died in A.D. 814), this elaborated form of the creed — now in the form we know as the Apostles' Creed — was received back in Rome.

So the Apostles' Creed has been used for well over a thousand years. It was accepted and used in the medieval

Western church and by the sixteenth-century Reformers and is used today by both Roman Catholics and Protestants.

To anyone who asks, "Why bother with the Apostles' Creed?" we would answer, first, that it is a concise but comprehensive summary of New Testament teaching and as such an invaluable aid toward a reasonably clear understanding of the Christian faith. Such clarity of understanding on the part of ordinary church members can seldom have been more urgently needed than it is today, when the complexity of life and the speed at which social, political, economic, and technological changes take place have increased so bewilderingly. Without this clarity how can Christians hope to keep their bearings? But no one can affirm that members with a really clear and coherent grasp of the gospel are common in our churches today.

We would also answer that the Apostles' Creed can fulfill a vital role as a rallying point when the church is under attack or — what is often more dangerous — ignored as irrelevant or patronized as a harmless curiosity. In Germany before 1933 it was customary in Protestant churches for the minister alone to recite the Creed in the Sunday service. But after 1933 congregations began to join in the recitation. Church members wanted this opportunity, in the face of Nazi attacks on the church, to confess their faith personally and publicly. What unites Christians of different traditions, languages, and nations and of different generations and centuries is a more effective and powerful vehicle of such confession than any occasional statement composed by an individual, however gifted, or by any particular denomination or group of Christians.

It would be salutary if, in those churches in which the Creed is regularly used, it were recited not perfunctorily but with deepened understanding and renewed confidence. It would also be health-giving for those churches in which the Creed is seldom if ever used to discover the thrill and inspiration of confessing together our common faith in a formula that binds us to our fellow Christians across denominational and national boundaries and across the centuries.

But the Creed must be studied and pondered. Its affirmations should be neither accepted nor rejected uncritically and without careful thought. It must be understood in the light of the whole witness of the Bible. And we will certainly not have understood it if we fail to see its relevance to the life of the modern world and to all the problems which that world presents.

– 2 –

I Believe

The meaning of "I believe" at the beginning of the Creed is determined by everything that follows those first words. It is whom we believe in that is decisive about Christian faith.* It is not our action of believing but the One in whom we believe, who he is and what he has done, is doing, and will do, God himself in his grace and his self-revelation, that is all-important. There is therefore much to be said for postponing discussion of "I believe" until after we have considered the rest of the Creed. But for the sake of convenience we will consider it now, even though this means that the basis and full significance of some statements that we need to make now will only begin to become clear as we go further into the Creed.

Faith is *God's gift*. We do not attain to faith by our efforts or cleverness or by being especially good or naturally pious. Faith is not a contribution we make from our side that establishes some sort of claim on God. God him-

---

* "Faith" rather than "belief" will generally be used in this book as the noun corresponding to the verb "believe."

self makes us open to the gospel. He creates and sustains faith. Faith is God's free and undeserved gift.

And yet, at the same time, faith is *a real personal decision on the part of the one who believes.* God himself gives us the possibility of making a truly personal decision, and the decision that we make on the basis of that God-given possibility is particularly the free personal decision of each one of us. We have here already one of the paradoxes of Christian theology.

The decision that has to be made is not between having a god and not having a god. That choice is not open to us. For, as Karl Barth pointed out, "There is no man who does not have his own god or gods as the object of his highest desire and trust, or as the basis of his deepest loyalty and commitment."* The choice to be made is, rather, between believing in the one true living God, the only real God, or believing in one or more of the false gods, behind all of which looms in the background the ultimate idol, each man's or woman's own ego. Faith of a sort we do indeed all have. But the "I believe" of the Creed means *a turning from false gods and a choosing the one and only real God.*

Faith is also *freedom.* To have faith is to be set free more and more from slavery to false gods and from self-tyranny and to be set free for the true God. To belong gladly to that God is the only true freedom.

And this freedom for God, which faith is, is also a beginning of being able to obey God. Faith is response to God's word, to the message that God has addressed to us. It means humbly submitting to accept his forgiveness and

* *Evangelical Theology: An Introduction* (1963), p. 3(1).

judgment and to recognize his claim on us, his right to our selves. So faith is *obedience*.

Faith is also *trust*, reliance on God's faithfulness. Weak and faltering though it may be, it is always directed toward becoming a full and perfect confidence in God.

Faith is *exclusive*. The trust, loyalty, and obedience that we owe to God we owe to him alone. He brooks no rival claims. As the Scots Confession of 1560 has it, "We . . . acknowledge one only God, to whom only we must cleave, whom only we must serve, whom only we must worship, and in whom only we must put our trust."

But faith, though it is trust, is no mere leap in the dark, a blind trust that asks no questions. For faith is *knowledge and understanding*. While the church recognizes that human reason is fallen like all else that is human, it refuses, wherever it is true to the Bible, to disparage reason or encourage anti-intellectualism, and it seeks seriously and strenuously to comprehend the gospel as clearly and coherently as possible. We must try to know the truth about God as fully as he allows us, to learn ever more and more about his character, his deeds, his ways, and his will, and to understand everything around us in the light of his truth. Proper worship includes learning more about God. With the recognition that faith is knowledge goes the realization that the gospel is truth and that a piety and a worship that are not deeply concerned about truth are abhorrent to the God of the Bible. (But it is important not to mistake for this proper recognition of faith as knowledge the sort of barren intellectualism against which James 2:19 warns.)

Faith is also *confession*. Faith must become public. The Creed was from the beginning a confession. We give public expression to our faith by playing our part in the church's public worship, in its mission, and in its practical service to the poor and to those who are otherwise disadvantaged and by witnessing as individuals to the truth of the gospel in word and deed. This witness includes the fulfillment of our political responsibility, which is particularly great for those of us who live in democracies.

Finally, the statement in Acts 16:34 that the Philippian jailer "and his entire household rejoiced that he had become a believer in God" points to the fact that faith of the sort to which the Creed gives expression is always, however much it may be accompanied by troubles, pains, and griefs, *a source of joy* — true, deep, and lasting joy.

– 3 –

In God, the Father Almighty

To understand the words "God the Father," we again have to anticipate what will be said later in the Creed. The Creed does not speak of God as "Father" in some general sort of way. There is nothing here like the Homeric phrase "father both of men and of gods," used of Zeus, the high god of the ancient Greeks. The Creed speaks, rather, of God as the Father of "Jesus Christ, his only Son." So it is necessary at this point to say something about the Christian doctrine of the Trinity.

When the Creed speaks of "God the Father," "his only Son," and "the Holy Spirit," it is not speaking of three gods, but of the one and only true God, who in his eternal being is the Father, the Son, and the Holy Spirit. Sometimes Christians, in their anxiety to assert emphatically the divinity of Christ and the Holy Spirit, fall into ways of speaking of the Persons of the Trinity that suggest the existence of three gods. But the Christian doctrine of the Trinity is certainly not a doctrine of three gods or a tritheism. That there is only one true God is every bit as important to Christians as it is to Jews.

But it must be admitted that the use of "person" in

this connection is, in spite of its long and respectable history, likely to be misleading for people of today. We normally use "person" to denote an individual, a separate and independent self. But the Persons of the Trinity are not three separate individuals or selves. They are, rather, the three ways in which God exists, the three ways in which the one God is God. It is God's revelation of himself that compels us to know him as the Trinity.

But that he is the one God as Father, Son, and Holy Spirit is a matter not just of how he has revealed himself but also of how he is in himself. Christians believe that God is — not just in the process of his self-revelation but also in himself eternally — the Father, the Son, and the Holy Spirit. The fact of this threefold life of God explains why 1 John 4:8 and 16 can say truly that "God is love," implying that he has always been love, even before the creation existed. It is because he has always in his oneness had this eternally threefold life that he has never been lonely, but has always loved, quite independently of creation being there to be loved. In himself in the eternal threefoldness of his own life he is eternally love.

When the Creed speaks of God as "Father," the reference is primarily to the fact that the one God is, in himself and from all eternity, the Father of his only Son. It is the eternal Son alone who is Son of God by right. The phrase "Father of our Lord Jesus Christ" occurs quite often in the New Testament.

But we also affirm that God is, for the sake of his only Son, *our* Father. This fatherhood of God in relation to us is not at all natural or necessary. It is, rather, a matter of sheer grace, the stupendous grace of the eternal God, who adopts human beings as his sons and daughters for the sake of his own dear Son and gives them the right to call him "Father."

[13]

This Christian belief in God as our Father is something altogether different from all ideas that derive only from our own wishful thinking, whether of a kindly disposed and powerful divine protector to counter our sense of insecurity, or of a patriarchal authority figure to be the sanction of the diverse sorts of human authority that we either submit to (more or less willingly) or ourselves exercise.

It is only those whom the Holy Spirit enables to believe in Jesus Christ who have the privilege of *knowing* that they are God's adopted sons and daughters and that they have the right and the duty to address God as "Father" with humble confidence. But is God also for Christ's sake the Father of all other human beings, even though this is unrecognized by them? Should they, too, be recognized by Christians as adopted children of God, however deeply unaware they may be of what Christ has done for them? The wisest response to these questions is the counsel that John Calvin gives in his discussion of the word "our" at the beginning of the Lord's Prayer: The Christian should in his (or her) prayers "embrace all who are his brothers in Christ, not only those whom he at present sees and recognizes as such but all men [and women] who dwell on earth. For what God has determined concerning them is beyond our knowing except that it is no less godly than humane to wish and hope the best for them."*

*   *   *

In describing God the Father as "almighty," the Creed contrasts him as supremely strong and incomparably

Institutes of the Christian Religion III.xx.38, as translated by F. L. Battles and edited by J. T. McNeill (1960).

powerful with all weakness, both obvious weakness and weakness that for a time passes as strength. Power is indeed so characteristic of God that the word "power" can be used in the New Testament as a way of referring to God (Mark 14:62, where RSV and NRSV rightly capitalize "Power").

God's power is utterly real, unfailing, and perfect, but it is not absolute or unqualified. It is determined and limited by the character of the One who is almighty. God "cannot deny himself" (2 Timothy 2:13). All notions of God's almightiness as being indeterminate, absolute power, the ability to do just anything, are once and for all excluded.

So the Bible, on the one hand, strains the capacity of human language in its attempts to express the incomparable greatness of God's power (e.g., Job 38; Psalm 145; Isaiah 40:21-31; Matthew 10:29-30; Romans 8:28), and, on the other hand, makes it abundantly clear that the power that it ascribes to him is the power of the One who is altogether righteous, merciful, and faithful. With the word "almighty" we confess that God the Father is able to accomplish perfectly what he wills, his own righteous and merciful purposes. But he is unable to contradict his own character and so respects both the real measure of freedom that he has given to his human creatures, whose voluntary obedience he desires, and also the orderliness and consistency of his universe. Therefore, we should not be surprised that the working out of his gracious purposes is often painfully obscure to us, that our patience is often tried to the limit, and that belief in God as both good and almighty is often exceedingly difficult.

[15]

– 4 –

Creator of Heaven and Earth

In this phrase of the Creed we affirm our belief that God the Father Almighty (our faith in whom we have just confessed) is the Creator. The Creed is not expressing a general religious conviction, common to all theists, that the existence of the universe implies the existence of a creator, but is acknowledging truth learned from God's self-revelation in Jesus Christ and in the Bible's attestation of Christ. The first article of the Creed is not, in this phrase any more than in the preceding one, attempting to lay a foundation of generally agreed religion on which a specifically Christian superstructure can then be built in the second article, when we begin to speak of Christ. What is affirmed here is already a specifically Christian faith in God as Creator. The starting point for understanding is not the existence of this world with all its multiplicity of life and of the universe of which it is a relatively tiny part, but the reality of God — Father, Son, and Holy Spirit. From this starting point and in this light, we begin to glimpse something of the true meaning of the existence of reality other than God.

The words "heaven" and "earth" are used variously in Scripture, but here, used together, they signify the whole of what exists besides God. The Nicene Creed rightly clarifies the meaning by adding "and of all things visible and invisible." By calling God the Father "creator of heaven and earth" we are affirming that he is the sole originator of all reality other than himself. He has not, like a craftsman, fashioned it out of some already existing material, but has created all things out of nothing.

We believe that God, constrained by no need, necessity, or loneliness, being eternally rich, blessed, and perfect in himself, of his pure grace, his love, which knows no cause outside itself, decided in his freedom not to be for himself alone but to create human beings to be the witnesses, and the whole universe to be the theater, of his glory. It is God's gracious covenant with humankind, established by the divine plan that the eternal Son should take on himself our nature, that is the inmost meaning of God's creation of heaven and earth.

According to the Scriptures it was by his Word, that Word which in the fullness of time was to assume human nature for humankind's sake, that God created all things. And it is by that same Word that he preserves all things in existence and keeps them in order (John 1:3, 10; Colossians 1:16-17; Hebrews 1:2-3; 11:3).

We have now seen something of what we are affirming about God by the words "creator of heaven and earth." But the words are also an affirmation about humankind, since humankind is part of what has been created. We acknowledge in the Creed that we are God's creatures and that to try to understand the meaning of our existence apart from his existence is vain. To deny our creatureliness, to imagine that we are the center and the measure of all things, existing for ourselves, is to be out of touch with reality and caught in a world of illusion.

To attempt in this way to usurp God's place, to live a self-centered life, is the essence of sin (Genesis 3:5). It is to succumb to the lie of idolatry, the great comprehensive falsehood. The ultimate idol lurking behind, above, and under all other idols is each person's own self trying to usurp the place of God. Since we are all sinners, people who have exchanged the truth of God for the lie of our self-centeredness, our lives are subject to futility. But God's gracious purpose for us is that we should possess and sustain our true dignity as creatures meant to be conscious and intelligent witnesses of his work, created to know, glorify, and enjoy him forever.

With our confession of God as creator we are also affirming something about the universe apart from us, the whole of nonhuman creation, animate and inanimate. We are affirming that it is, in fact, God's creation and that as such it has its own inalienable worth and dignity. We thus acknowledge the obligation that rests on us to respect and defend its dignity. We are confessing that the whole inanimate universe was created to be the theater of God's glory, in which the drama of God's praise is to be enacted, and that all the manifold life of nonhuman animate nature has its functions to fulfill as a magnificent chorus in the drama in which humanity as the chief actor has its own special, rational part to play.

This means that we are forbidden to think of nature, whether animate or inanimate, as merely materials to be exploited at will for our use, convenience, or pleasure. To recognize that God created heaven and earth is to know that it is not only for the sake of our fellow human beings, whether of today or of generations to come, that we must refrain from spoiling the natural world. We must also, because of that confession, respect and defend the natural

[18]

world for its own sake as God's creation, for which he cares, to which he is "a faithful Creator" (1 Peter 4:19), and over which his promise stands that at last it, too, will be set free to "obtain the freedom of the glory of the children of God" (Romans 8:21), the freedom, that is, to fulfill fully and perfectly its Creator's purpose for it. But it cannot have that freedom as long as humanity refuses to play its own part in the great drama of God's praise.

It goes without saying that the first chapters of Genesis were not intended to be a matter-of-fact account of the origin of the universe and of life within it. They are, rather, a poetic-theological statement of the why, whence, and whither of the universe and life, a marvelously suggestive and illuminating statement that is full of profound truth. Faith in God as Creator of heaven and earth involves no denial of the propriety of scientific inquiry. In fact, it should encourage frank and fearless investigation of nature, so long as it respects creation's dignity and worth and does not wantonly damage or destroy, and so long as the knowledge gained is not exploited for evil ends. How far we are permitted to go in manipulating nature is sometimes difficult to know, and Christians will differ in the judgments they make. Reverence for God the Creator, for the rights of our fellow human beings of today and of the future, and for the dignity of all God's creatures, animate and inanimate — these should be our guides, and they will hold us back from all wasting and spoiling, from all cruelty to creatures capable of feeling, and from insatiable greed.

In Genesis 1 it is again and again said that God saw that what he had made was good (verses 4, 10, 12, 18, 21, 25, and, most emphatically, 31). In this phrase of the Creed we celebrate God's good creation. But to do so raises the problem of evil's presence in what God created good, which is a mystery that we cannot solve. A partial answer is no doubt seen in God's gift to human beings of freedom, a freedom that we can either use rightly or misuse. The story of the serpent's temptation of Eve is illuminating, and so is the whole account of the Fall, which sees non-human creation as sharing the baleful consequences of human disobedience (Genesis 3:17: "cursed is the ground because of you").

But we are still left asking why. In the light of Scripture, we cannot accept any attribution of evil to God, or any dualistic notion of a principle of evil in some measure balancing God, or any belittling of the the seriousness of evil. A simple and tidy solution cannot be given. But we shall see (in chapter 7, below) that Christians believe that God has dealt with evil by the cross of Christ.

– 5 –

I Believe in Jesus Christ,
His Only Son, Our Lord

The first and the third articles of the Apostles' Creed are properly understood only in the light of the second, the Creed's great middle section. It is only through Jesus Christ that we truly know God as the Father and as the Holy Spirit.

"Jesus" is the name of a man who belongs to human history, to a particular time and place. It is the Greek form of a Jewish name, "Joshua" or "Yeshua." Like some other names, it has a meaning: "Yahweh is salvation" or "salvation of Yahweh." In Jesus' day it was a common name among Jews, and Jesus of Nazareth was distinguished from other men with this name by the name of his hometown.

"Christ" is the Greek equivalent of Hebrew "Messiah," and means "anointed." During his ministry Jesus seems to have been reluctant to use the title of himself, presumably because he recognized the limitations and objectionable features of current Jewish messianic expectation. But he seems to have accepted on occasion, even if with reserve, its use with regard to him by others.

By its use of this title "Christ," the church confesses that Jesus is the true Messiah of Israel, the meaning and the fulfillment of the long succession of Israel's kings and priests, and the fulfillment of God's promises to Israel and of Israel's age-long hopes. The church also thus acknowledges the necessity of paying attention to the Old Testament's attestation of Christ, if we would know him as he truly is. It acknowledges also the special place of the Jews in God's plan of salvation, recognizing and accepting them as the kinsfolk of the one Jew, the universal Savior, in whom and for whose sake they were and, in spite of unbelief, disobedience, and rejection, still are — now in mysterious partnership with the church — God's special people.

*   *   *

That the New Testament bears witness to Jesus Christ as "his only Son," that is, as the Son of God, there can be no doubt. Paul writes that the Thessalonian Christians turned from idols to serve the true God "and to wait for his Son from heaven, . . . Jesus" (1 Thessalonians 1:10), that "God sent his Son" (Galatians 4:4; cf. Romans 8:3), that his own faith is in "the Son of God, who loved me and gave himself for me" (Galatians 2:20), that "the gospel of God" is "the gospel concerning his Son" (Romans 1:1, 3), that "we were reconciled to God through the death of his Son" (Romans 5:10), and that God "did not withhold his own Son, but gave him up for all of us" (Romans 8:32). Jesus as "God's Son" is also a constantly recurring theme in Mark, the earliest of the Gospels (1:1, 11; 3:11; 8:38; 9:7; 12:6; 13:32; 14:36, 61; 15:39). For the Gospel of John it is enough to refer to 1:14 and 18 and 3:16:

> And the Word became flesh and lived among us, and we have seen his glory, the glory as of the Father's only Son, full of grace and truth.

No one has ever seen God. It is the only Son, who is close to the Father's heart, who has made him known.

For God so loved the world that he gave his only Son, so that everyone who believes in him may not perish but have eternal life.

John 20:31 sets out the author's purpose in writing:

But these are written so that you may come to believe that Jesus is the Messiah, the Son of God, and that through believing you may have life in his name.

The words of the Creed, "his only Son," are vital for Christian faith. If what this three-word phrase affirms were untrue, there would be no gospel. The reality of the good news is altogether dependent on the truth of the claim that Mary's son, who was crucified under Pontius Pilate, was none other than God's only Son. Take away these three words from the Creed, and the whole falls apart.

But if these three words are true in their full and proper sense, as the fourth-century church sought through much debate and intellectual effort to define it against all tendencies and attempts to diminish, distort, or water it down,* then there is indeed a gospel, and the person and work of Jesus Christ is real help for us, because in him God himself has come in person to our aid, God's very self and no other. Since these three words of

*In the words of the Nicene Creed (381): "the only-begotten Son of God, begotten of the Father before all worlds, God of God, Light of Light, very God of very God, begotten, not made, being of one substance with the Father; by whom all things were made."

the Creed are really true, there is real revelation in Jesus Christ, because in him God himself was revealing himself through himself, and there is real deliverance for sinners, because God himself has taken our sins upon himself. We are in the presence of the ineffable grace and mystery that the eternal Son, who is inseparably one with the Father, has assumed our nature for the sake of us human beings and for our salvation, without ever ceasing to be eternal God.

*   *   *

The Creed adds "our Lord." The most important part of the background of Paul's and the earliest church's use of "Lord" in reference to Jesus was use of the same title in the Greek version of the Old Testament to represent the Hebrew divine name Yahweh (Jehovah). This is indicated by the fact that on a number of occasions Paul applies to Christ Old Testament verses or phrases in which it is clear that "the Lord" is God himself (for example, Romans 10:13; 1 Thessalonians 5:2; and 2 Thessalonians 2:2). The early Christian creed "Jesus is Lord" (Romans 10:9; 1 Corinthians 12:3; 2 Corinthians 4:5; Philippians 2:11) therefore accorded to the exalted Jesus the name, majesty, and authority of God himself.

But, where "our" (as here in the Creed) or "my" precedes "Lord," a further thought is expressed: Christ has claimed us for his own and by his saving work has taken possession of us, and we respond by personal commitment to him in trust, loyalty, and obedience. It is this thought that finds memorable expression in the first question and answer of the Heidelberg Catechism: "What is your only comfort in life and in death? That I, both body and soul, in life and in death, am not my own but belong to my faithful Savior Jesus Christ. . . ."*

* The Heidelberg Catechism was composed by German Reformed Christians in 1563.

– 6 –

He Was Conceived by the Power of the Holy Spirit and Born of the Virgin Mary

Many Christians today have trouble affirming the virgin birth of Jesus. This is understandable. But the confidence with which some take it for granted that no thinking modern person could possibly accept the virgin birth as historical is quite unjustified. It is clear that the historicity of the virgin birth cannot be proven, but equally clear that it has not been disproved. And there are, in fact, weighty considerations in its favor.

None of the main arguments urged against the virgin birth, when examined carefully, is as strong as some have claimed. First, it is often said that in the New Testament only Matthew and Luke attest the virgin birth. But Mark (6:3) and John (1:13; 6:41-42; 8:41) probably reflect knowledge of the virgin birth tradition. Furthermore, it may well be significant that in Romans 1:3; Galatians 4:4; and Philippians 2:7 Paul avoids using with reference to the birth of Jesus the Greek verb that would be expected — which would have suggested the involvement of a human father — and instead uses a verb that does not carry that connotation (rendered in NRSV in the first of these three verses as "be descended" and in the other two as "be born").

Second, it is said that the genealogies in Matthew 1 and Luke 3 are witnesses against the historicity of the virgin birth, since they trace the ancestry of Jesus through Joseph. But Joseph was, in any case, Jesus' legal father, having acknowledged him by giving him his name (Matthew 1:25). It is in the light of this that the references (direct and indirect) to Jesus as Joseph's son in Matthew 13:55; Luke 2:33, 41, 43, 48; 4:22 are to be understood. The genealogies represent this legal parentage because the early church had a strong interest in establishing Jesus' Davidic descent in view of the widespread expectation that the Messiah would be of David's family.

Third, the apparent absence of any special understanding of Jesus during his ministry on the part of Mary and her family is alleged to be inconsistent with the historicity of the virgin birth. But, if the birth of Jesus was as Matthew and Luke indicate, it is surely likely that Joseph and Mary would have been reticent about it even within their own home, knowing that the truth would be bound to meet incredulity and reproach. And there is little reason for assuming that it would have rendered them immune from misunderstanding Jesus.

Fourth, it is often suggested that the Immanuel prophecy in Isaiah 7:14 was the origin of belief in the virgin birth. But there is no evidence that Isaiah 7:14 was understood in pre-Christian Judaism to refer to the Messiah or to foretell a virginal conception. The Hebrew word translated as "virgin" in the older English versions simply denotes a young woman. The Greek version of the verse (and the Greek version of the Old Testament was widely known) would hardly suggest the idea of a virginal conception to anyone who had not already got the idea from somewhere else, though, using as it does a Greek word that properly denotes a virgin, it was undoubtedly a welcome scriptural confirmation for those who already believed in the virgin birth.

Fifth, it is claimed that there is a wealth of parallels from ancient paganism that make acceptance of the historicity of the virgin birth impossible. But when these alleged parallels are examined, it becomes clear that none of them is a real parallel. In none of them is there any question of a truly virginal conception; the thought is rather of physical intercourse between a god and a woman that results in a birth. What is attested in Matthew and Luke is, by contrast, a divine act of creation. In fact, the more closely these supposed parallels are examined, the more clearly the contrast between them and the narratives in Matthew and Luke stands out. But enough superficial resemblance between these pagan stories and what the Gospels relate existed to have been a good reason for the church's reticence about the virgin birth. The church may well have sensed that the virgin birth, if proclaimed to the Gentile world, would probably be misunderstood as being like the birth of Perseus or Heracles or as a flattering fancy like the tales of the births of Plato, Alexander, or Augustus. This may help to account for the fewness of New Testament references to the virgin birth.

Sixth, at the back of many people's minds is the assumption that miracles do not happen, and that, since the virgin birth would be a miracle, it cannot have happened. But to maintain this as a matter of principle is hardly consistent either with belief in a Creator God or, indeed, with the position of an agnostic.

That Jesus was not Joseph's physical son seems virtually certain. For one thing, two mutually hostile traditions, the Christian and the Jewish traditions, both agree that he was not (the Jews maintaining that he was Mary's son by another man). For another thing, it is surely impossible to suppose that Christians simply invented the virgin birth (either of their own initiative or in response to Jewish slander), knowing all the time that Jesus really was Joseph's son, when we take into account the following facts: that the earliest church was convinced that Jesus was the Messiah; that there was no pre-Christian expectation that the Messiah would be virgin-born; that there was a very strong, even if not universal, expectation that the Messiah would be a descendant of David; and that the Davidic descent of Joseph was asserted.

We have to choose between only two alternatives: Either Jesus was the son of Mary and of some man other than Joseph, or he was born of Mary when she was a virgin. We cannot hope to make an absolutely certain decision between these two possibilities from a purely historical point of view. But the arguments urged against the historicity of the virgin birth are by no means as cogent as has often been assumed. Furthermore, the fact that no one has produced a really convincing explanation of how belief in the virgin birth arose, under the assumption that it is not historical, is a strong ground for accepting its truth.

*　　*　　*

If then we accept the truth of the virgin birth (as the present writer does), what does it mean?

First, while the virgin birth does not prove the truth of the incarnation and while we must not say that God was unable to effect the incarnation in some other way, the virgin birth does point to the mystery of the personal union of God and humanity in Jesus Christ. To confess

[29]

that Jesus Christ was "born of the Virgin Mary" is to recognize the mystery as mystery.

Second, the Creed's affirmation that Jesus Christ "was conceived by the power of the Holy Spirit" (cf. Matthew 1:18; Luke 1:35) means that God himself made a new beginning in the history of his creation by coming in person and becoming part of that history. He himself originated this particular human life, that of Jesus, by a new act of creation. Therefore, Jesus Christ is not a savior emerging from the continuity of our human history, but God in person intervening in history from outside history.

Third, that Jesus was "born of . . . Mary" means that he is truly human. The eternal Word really did assume our nature. While remaining what he always was, he became a true human being.

Finally, that Jesus' mother was a virgin attests that God's redemption is "by grace alone." Here our humanity, represented by Mary, does nothing more than accept, than submit to being simply the object of God's grace. That is the real significance of the address "favored one" to Mary in Luke 1:28. The male, characteristically the dominant and aggressive element of humanity, is excluded from this action and set aside, and in Mary our humanity's part is simply to be made the receptacle of God's gift, the object of God's mercy: "Here am I, the servant of the Lord; let it be with me according to your word" (Luke 1:38).

He Suffered under Pontius Pilate, Was Crucified, Died, and Was Buried. He Descended to the Dead

It is a striking feature of the Creed that immediately after "born of the Virgin Mary" comes "suffered under Pontius Pilate." The fifty-fifth question and answer of Calvin's Geneva Catechism of 1541 are as follows: "Why do you go immediately from his birth to his death, passing over the whole history of his life? Because nothing is said here but what pertains properly to the substance of our redemption." Karl Barth was surely right to see this as unsatisfactory.* Can we really believe that Jesus' life between his birth and his death did not belong to the substance of our redemption? Barth rightly preferred the corresponding passage in the Heidelberg Catechism of 1563: "What do you understand by the word 'Suffered'? That all the time of his life on earth, but especially at the end of it, he bore, in body and soul, the wrath of God against the sin of the whole human race. . . ."

The Creed, with "suffered under Pontius Pilate," is no doubt focusing attention on the end of Christ's earthly life (most of his life was, of course, not lived under Pilate's

---

Dogmatics in Outline (1949), pp. 101ff.

governorship of Judea), but it was a sound theological perception on the part of the two authors of the Heidelberg Catechism that recognized the appropriateness of "suffered" as a description of the whole of Christ's life. The suffering that reached its fearful climax in the Passion characterized the whole of his life. We may think here of the poverty surrounding his birth, the hardships of his life in Nazareth, the lack of success that, for the most part, marked his ministry, and the restraints and frustrations of that messianic "veiledness" to which in obedience to his Father he had to submit. Through it all he was carrying our burdens.

Pilate was an unsavory character and in himself not a weighty historical figure. But mention of his name in the Creed serves two purposes. First, it dates the Passion of Jesus (Pilate was prefect of Judea A.D. 26-36), indicating that God's saving act was accomplished in our history, in the same continuity of history in which all of us live. Secondly, it marks the connection between that saving act and the institution of civil government. Pilate's name in the Creed is a constant reminder to Christians that all state power — and in a democracy that includes to some extent the whole electorate — stands under God's judgment. Human governments are very often guilty of injustice, like Pilate, who was unjust even by his own standards, since he delivered Jesus to execution to safeguard his own position after pronouncing him innocent. But Pilate's name in the Creed is also a reminder that the state stands under God's promise, since it is God's ordinance, ordained by him for his own merciful purposes, and those exercising authority are his servants (Romans 13:1-7; 1 Timothy 2:1-6) and are bound to further, consciously or unconsciously, willingly or unwillingly, directly or indirectly, his purposes. For through

Pilate, unworthy and unwilling servant though he was, God's perfect will for the redemption of humanity was accomplished.

*   *   *

The event recorded in "was crucified, died" was, in the first place and most importantly, God's saving act. God himself acted in this event, and he acted decisively to save. There he took to himself the whole burden of human sin, the guilt, shame, and grief, and the dreadful weight of his own wrath against sin, and bore it all for us and in our stead in order to pardon us righteously and lovingly, without in any way condoning our sin. A divine forgiveness on any cheaper terms would have meant God's abandonment of his faithful love of us and the destruction of our true dignity as God's morally accountable creatures. In the cross God worked out for us his costly forgiveness, bearing the full cost of it himself.

It is of most vital importance that we recognize that it was God himself, and none other, who bore the cost. To think of Jesus as a third party besides God and sinful humanity, an innocent third party punished for the sins of humankind, would be to attribute to God an act of fearful horror. God did not lay the burden of our iniquities on a third party, but on himself— on his very self— in that human nature that his own dear Son, who is eternally God, inseparably one with the Father and the Holy Spirit, had for our sakes assumed. We must never forget that it is only within the framework of a proper trinitarian doctrine of God that the cross can be rightly understood.

In the second place, the cross was the revelation of God's wrath. How terrible that wrath is we are not allowed to see except in the event in which God himself directs it on himself and removes it from us. But in his act of dealing with our sin he does let us know how seriously he hates our sin.

This is the meaning of Jesus' fear in the face of his approaching death (Mark 14:33), about which Luther could say, "No one ever feared death so much as this Man."* It is the meaning of the awful gulf that opens, not between God and sinners, but within the essential and unbroken unity of the personal existence of the one eternal God himself, when Jesus cries, "My God, my God, why have you forsaken me?" (Mark 15:34).

If this wrath of God against all evil were not real, God would not be the good, loving, and merciful God that he is. It is because he truly loves us seriously and faithfully that he responds to our sin with wrath and relentless resistance. His wrath is not contrary to his faithful love. It is, rather, an expression of that love. That God's wrath, as the wrath of him who is perfectly good, is free from everything that compromises and disfigures our so-called "righteous indignation," even at its very best and most credible, should go without saying.

In the third place, the cross unmasked the real nature of human sin as the sordid, squalid, ugly, and futile thing that it always is, as the human attempt to suppress God's truth and bury it out of sight because it gives the lie to every human being's illusion that his or her own self is God. At the cross our enmity to God is laid bare. We do our worst there to God, and none of us can disown as altogether alien from himself or herself the attitudes and actions of Annas, Caiaphas, the scribes and Pharisees, Pilate, and the Jerusalem multitude. They represent us all.

*Weimar edition of Luther's works, XXXVII, 326.

*　　*　　*

The words "and was buried" have their own importance, since burial is the seal of the fact of death. All four Gospels record Jesus' burial, as does the summary of early teaching repeated by Paul in 1 Corinthians 15 (verse 4).

The Reformed catechisms tend to explain "He descended to the dead" as a reference to Christ's bearing "unspeakable anguish, pains, and terrors . . . in his life and especially on the cross" (Heidelberg Catechism, question 44). But in the early church these words were understood as referring to the time between Christ's death and resurrection, during which he was among the dead, his body in the tomb but his spirit alive (cf. 1 Peter 3:18b-20; 4:6; also Acts 2:27, 31; Romans 10:7; Ephesians 4:8-10). That this clause follows "and was buried" lends some support to this interpretation of the Creed. Should we perhaps see particularly in 1 Peter 3 a hint that the period between the first Good Friday afternoon and early on Easter Sunday was not void of redemptive significance?

– 8 –

On the Third Day He Rose Again

That the resurrection of Christ is of central importance in the New Testament is not to be doubted. For Paul belief that God raised Jesus from the dead is what distinguishes Christians from other people: "if you confess with your lips that Jesus is Lord and believe in your heart that God raised him from the dead, you will be saved" (Romans 10:9). The author of Acts can refer to the preaching of the apostles in the earliest days of the church as "their testimony to the resurrection of the Lord Jesus" (Acts 4:33). For the New Testament the affirmation that Jesus was raised on the third day is that by which the church stands or falls. "If Christ has not been raised," says Paul in 1 Corinthians 15:14, "then our proclamation has been in vain and your faith has been in vain."

We do not have to look for a special significance of Easter distinct from that of Good Friday. The significance of Easter is that it validates what was accomplished on Good Friday as God's own saving deed by confirming that the one who was crucified really is God's "only Son." For the Christian the resurrection is God's seal on Jesus' work on the cross. The vital question is, then, "Is it true?"

The most persuasive objection to the Creed's affirmation of the resurrection is the apparent sheer incredibleness of the claim that a man who was really and truly dead was raised to life. But this objection, though enough to convince very many that the Christian claim is illusory, is clearly not a conclusive disproof of its truth.

The other main objection is that there are a number of apparent discrepancies between the different accounts in the Gospels and 1 Corinthians of the incidents associated with the resurrection (the New Testament has no narrative of the actual raising of Jesus). Most of the discrepancies seem to be of the sort that is common enough wherever there are several accounts of one incident and are therefore not particularly significant. Such is the case with the discrepancies regarding when the women would seem to have prepared their spices and ointments, when they went to the tomb, how many women there were, and what their names were. But there are four apparent discrepancies that require closer examination.

First, in contrast with all four Gospels, Paul says nothing about a visit of women (or a woman) to the tomb. But there is no need to infer that he was unaware of the part played by the women. He probably omitted mention of them in 1 Corinthians 15:4ff. because he wanted to cite only witnesses who would be generally acceptable as witnesses. Women were not accepted as credible witnesses in Jewish legal practice.

Second, while all the Gospels refer to the empty tomb, Paul does not mention the tomb at all. But this is probably simply a consequence of his omitting the women as witnesses.

Third, 1 Corinthians 15:5 and Luke 24:34 seem to imply that the first person to see the risen Jesus was Peter, but Matthew 28:9 and John 20:14-17 agree that Jesus appeared first either to Mary Magdalene alone or to her and "the other Mary." Again, we should probably recognize in 1 Corinthians and Luke the effect of concern that the testimony should be generally acceptable.

Fourth, while Matthew and John record appearances of the risen Jesus both in Jerusalem and in Galilee, Luke records appearances only in and near Jerusalem. Furthermore, by his omission of any parallel to Mark 14:28, his alteration of Mark 16:7 (in Luke 24:6f.), and his inclusion of the command to tarry in Jerusalem in 24:49, Luke seems to exclude all thought of a Galilean appearance.* (Mark's position with regard to this question is problematic, since Mark 16:9-20 is generally agreed to be a later addition to the Gospel.) But there seems to be no cogent reason why we should not suppose that the risen Jesus appeared both in and near Jerusalem and also in Galilee.

A number of considerations must be mentioned as strongly supporting the truth of the resurrection. First is the astounding transformation of the disciples from the frightened, discouraged men depicted in, for example, Mark 14:50, 66-72; John 20:19 into the bold and energetic witnesses of a risen Christ that they were within a few weeks of the crucifixion. Such a change implies a sufficient cause. This the resurrection of Jesus would have been.

Second, neither the Jewish nor the Roman authorities ever produced evidence to disprove the claim that Jesus had been raised. This is highly significant. The Jewish authorities in particular had every reason to want to bring

*The usual assumption of scholars is that the authors of Luke and Matthew made use of the Gospel of Mark as they wrote their Gospels.

forth such evidence, and they must surely have been in a position to search and interrogate thoroughly. They must have known within a few days of the crucifixion what the disciples were saying, and the chances of finding the body, if the claim that Jesus had been raised was not true, must surely have been good. They must have known that to produce the body would be the most effective way of destroying what to them was a dangerous movement. That they never did produce it is surely a most important point in favor of the truth of the resurrection.

Third, there is Paul's conversion. This ardent persecutor of the disciples was certainly not predisposed to accept the truth of the resurrection. To accept it entailed for him a personally humiliating about-face. He was closely associated with the Jewish authorities and so must have been familiar with their views concerning Jesus' ministry and the subsequent events. Moreover, he was clearly a man of great intelligence and learning, not the sort of person to be taken in easily. His conversion and subsequent career are especially impressive evidence for the truth of the resurrection.

Fourth, Jewish Christians, as well as Gentile Christians, soon came to observe the first day of the week as the special day for Christian worship. They did this in spite of all that the sabbath meant to Jews and in spite of Jesus' observance of the sabbath all his life. This suggests strongly that they were convinced that something had happened on the first day of the week of such altogether transcendent importance as to take precedence even over that which the sabbath celebrated.

Fifth, the striking prominence of women in the Gospel Easter narratives is inexplicable except as authentic historical memory. It is surely inconceivable that the early

Christian community would have invented traditions that paid no attention to accepted Jewish views about credible witnesses, that (in the circumstances of the time) would have been liable to attract ridicule, and that, moreover, were contrary to the natural tendency of the church to magnify the apostles — representing, as those traditions do, the women as receiving the news of the resurrection before any of the apostles.

Sixth, the existence of the church through more than nineteen and a half centuries carries at least some weight as evidence for the truth of the claim that on the third day Christ was raised from the dead.

The claim that it is possible to believe in Jesus' resurrection without believing that his dead body was raised has recently attracted much attention. But that understanding of the resurrection is not belief in the resurrection as attested by the New Testament. It is true that Paul does not mention the empty tomb in 1 Corinthians 15, but that is because he omits the women's visit to the tomb, preferring to list only male witnesses. And the sequence "died . . . was buried . . . was raised" in 1 Corinthians 15:3-4 implies the empty tomb, as does Paul's use there and elsewhere of the words "raise" and "resurrection."

At the same time the idea that after the resurrection Jesus' body possessed exactly the same properties as it had before death must also be rejected as inconsistent with the New Testament witness. Jesus is portrayed as freely appearing and vanishing, as becoming less or more recognizable, and apparently as unhindered by closed doors (Luke 24:16, 31; John 20:14-16, 19, 26). The New Testament indicates that after the resurrection he had the same body as the one that was crucified, but also that it had

[40]

come to be wonderfully transformed into a glorious body no longer subject to the limitations of earthly life.

*   *   *

In the end there seem to be only four possibilities from which to choose regarding the affirmation that Jesus was raised from the dead:

- that it originated in a fraud,
- that it originated in a mistake,
- that it originated in a combination of fraud and mistake, or
- that it is true.

Matthew 27:62-66 and 28:11-15 are evidence that the explanation of the resurrection as a fraud perpetrated by the disciples was current among Jews when Matthew's Gospel was written. But what motives could there have been for such a fraud? What chances would it have had of succeeding? Would not the perpetrators of a concerted deception have taken more care to make their stories agree? Would a fraud have produced the transformation of the disciples that actually took place? Can responsibility for such a fraud be reconciled with what is known of the character and conduct of the earliest Christians? Hardly easier to accept is the supposition that the church's belief rests ultimately on a mistake, whether it be that Jesus' followers looked for his body in the wrong tomb or that the resurrection appearances were hallucinations mistaken for reality. Is not the fourth alternative — that Jesus really was raised from the dead — difficult to accept though it may be, by far the least incredible alternative?

Positive and conclusive proof of the resurrection by scientific, historical, or other scholarly means is not to be had. But we may believe that Jesus was raised from the dead without in any way violating our intellectual and moral integrity.

9

He Ascended into Heaven, and Is Seated
at the Right Hand of the Father

Here we have two statements, one referring to the past, the last of the series that began with "He was conceived by the power of the Holy Spirit," the other referring to the present.

The New Testament speaks of Christ ascending (John 3:13; 20:17; Ephesians 4:10), being exalted (Acts 2:33; 5:31; Philippians 2:9), being taken up (Acts 1:2; 1 Timothy 3:16), going to the Father (John 14:12, 28), and going into heaven (1 Peter 3:22). What is related in Acts 1:9-11 is best understood as the mysterious ending of the last of the resurrection appearances, not as an actual description of Christ's return to the Father, which no mortal eye saw. But the manner in which the last resurrection appearance ended was a sign of that unseen event and a pointer to it. All the resurrection appearances ended with Christ vanishing. But there seems to have been something about the manner of his vanishing that last time that caused the disciples to understand both that they were not to expect him to appear again in this sort of way before his final coming and also that his departure was a departure to glory, his return to the Father.

Christ's ascension is, on the one hand, his departure

from his disciples. It thus fulfills his statement "you will not always have me" (Mark 14:7). It is when the time of his absence begins (Mark 13:34-36). During this time, though he keeps his promise to be with them always (Matthew 28:20), coming to them again and again through the Holy Spirit in the word and the sacraments and in the persons of his suffering brothers and sisters, he is not with them directly as he was during his earthly ministry and as he will be in the final reunion. During this time the church must "walk by faith, not by sight" (2 Corinthians 5:7).

The ascension is also Christ's entrance into the unrestricted freedom and effectiveness of his exalted life. It was surely some glimpsing of this truth that made the disciples return to Jerusalem after his departure, not with the sadness that might have been expected but, as Luke 24:52 says, "with great joy."

*   *   *

The second statement refers to the present. The picture language of sitting at the right hand — it should, of course, be recognized as picture language — is derived from the practice of oriental royal courts, in which the chief minister would sit or stand at the king's right hand and exercise the authority delegated to him. Use of this image in reference to the exalted Christ (e.g., Romans 8:34; Colossians 3:1) echoes its use in Psalm 110:1:

> The Lord says to my lord,
> "Sit at my right hand
> until I make your enemies your footstool."

The fact that this verse is quoted or echoed in the New

Testament more often than any other Old Testament verse and the fact that the earliest creed of the church seems to have been "Jesus is Lord" (see Romans 10:9; 1 Corinthians 12:3; 2 Corinthians 4:5; Philippians 2:11) suggest strongly that the focus of the earliest church's faith was the present lordship of the exalted Christ. Paul's determination to concentrate on Christ crucified (1 Corinthians 2:2) was not a determination to focus attention on Christ dying or dead, but to concentrate it on the Christ who had died on the cross but is now alive and exalted as Lord of all.

He who is now exalted possessed from all eternity, as the eternal Son of God, the glory and authority of his Father. What is new in his present sitting at his Father's right hand is that it is now as human, as our brother, that he possesses the glory, majesty, and power of God. For we believe that he is still human as well as divine, that in assuming our humanity he joined it to his divine nature forever.

*   *   *

The significance for us of the ascended Christ's sitting at the right hand of God is seen in three roles that he fulfills: as priest, as king, and as the one who prepares a place for us.

First, he is our High Priest, the one who has obtained forgiveness for us and made it possible for us sinners to approach God's holiness with confidence. As the Jewish high priest entered the holy of holies in the temple, so Christ has entered on our behalf into God's very presence. The Jewish high priest had to take with him the blood of an animal sacrifice to sprinkle on the mercy seat, but Christ has entered God's presence in the efficacy of his own death on the cross for the sins of all humanity. Unlike the Jewish high priest, Christ had no need to "offer sacrifice for his own sins as well as for those of the people" (Hebrews 5:3), since he is without sin. The Jewish high priest had to enter the holy of holies once every year, but Christ has entered into God's presence for us "once for all" (Hebrews 9:12; cf. 9:25f., 28). His sacrifice never has to be repeated, since he has offered, as the Book of Common Prayer puts it, "a full, perfect and sufficient sacrifice, oblation, and satisfaction, for the sins of the whole world."

And having dealt with the guilt and shame of our sin by bearing it for us, he is now forever "in the presence of God on our behalf" (Hebrews 9:24). He is there as our "advocate with the Father" (1 John 2:1), the one "who is at the right hand of God, who indeed intercedes for us" (Romans 8:34). And this High Priest of ours is one who understands our temptations and griefs from the inside, having experienced them himself, who can "sympathize with our weaknesses," "who in every respect has been tested as we are, yet without sin" (Hebrews 4:15).

But our High Priest does not only pray for us; he lives for us. The life that he lives at God's right hand is in a very real sense our true life. So Paul can say in Colossians 3:3, "your life is hidden with Christ in God." God in his mercy has decided to see us in his Son. This is what justification means, that God mercifully sees the sinful life that we have lived and are still living as a thing of the past — dead in Christ's death — and Christ's life as ours. Because this is so, we must and we may set our minds on Christ at the right hand of God and seek in our actual living to die daily and hourly to sin and to rise daily and hourly to newness of life in obedience to God.

Second, the ascended Christ is our King. "All authority in heaven and on earth" is his (Matthew 28:18). Hebrews 2:8 says that God has put "everything in subjection under his feet," but also admits that "we do not yet see everything in subjection to him" (RSV). His kingship is not yet acknowledged by all. It is still veiled and hidden in this world. But it is nonetheless real and irrevocable, and there is no doubt about the final outcome. In spite of everything that at present denies and mocks his kingship, "he must reign until he has put all his enemies under his feet" (1 Corinthians 15:25).

This Christ is King of the church. The church has no other king or head but Jesus Christ. It is through the witness of Scripture to him that he rules his people. Through that witness he engages his church in conversation with himself and makes his will known. The question that every church authority and every church member must answer with regard to every matter is: What do you seriously and responsibly, in the light of Holy Scripture, believe to be the will of Christ, the only King and Head of the church?

Christ is also King of the world, of the entire universe. The church is that part of his dominion in which his authority is already in some measure known and acknowledged. But beyond its borders his authority is no less real, though not yet recognized. Every earthly power is answerable to him. He is already, in the words of Revelation 1:5, "the ruler of the kings of the earth."

Ultimately, therefore, whether consciously or unconsciously, willingly or unwillingly, directly or indirectly, the governments of the nations serve his purposes. The great weight of evidence that seems to call this into question is not to be denied or belittled. In a world in which injustice, cruelty, and greed often seem triumphant it is hard indeed to hold fast to the truth of the biblical testimony to Christ

[47]

as "King of kings and Lord of lords" (Revelation 19:16). But the Christian will hold fast to it, even if sometimes he or she is forced to pray: "I believe; help my unbelief!" (Mark 9:24).

Third, the ascended Christ has gone to prepare a place for us (John 14:2). He has entered within the veil "as a forerunner on our behalf" (Hebrews 6:20). His present glory is the pledge of our future glory, of our sharing his glory. The answer to question 49 of the Heidelberg Catechism names as one benefit that we receive from Christ's ascension that it is "a sure pledge that He, as the Head, will also take us, His members, up to Himself."

10

He Will Come Again
to Judge the Living and the Dead

After the long series of past tense clauses beginning with "he was conceived" and the single present tense, "is seated," we now get a future tense clause: "He will come." As Christ is our past, the one whose earthly life and death of perfect obedience have taken the place of our sinful past, and as he is our present, the one in whose exalted life our true life is hidden with God, so is he also our future, the one in whose coming glory all our hopes will have their realization.

There is a well-known vantage point in the city of Bern, Switzerland, from which on a clear day one can see the mass of the Bernese Alps as a single line of snowy peaks. But within the heart of those mountains, what looked like a single line of peaks is seen to be a marvelous complexity of peaks and ridges, of perpetual snows and glaciers, of deep valleys and rushing streams, of waterfalls and alpine meadows. So the believers of the Old Testament, looking forward into the future, saw God's coming salvation as a single mighty saving act. But when Jesus came, he indicated to his disciples that, though they were indeed witnessing in his ministry, in his life and death and resurrection, what prophets and kings had longed to see, there was a fulfillment yet to come. There would be an interval between the kingdom come in his ministry and the kingdom's final consummation. What the disciples were seeing was a veiled revelation, recognizable only by faith, a revelation that could be rejected and denied. God was exercising his kingship in apparent weakness. But in the future what was veiled would be made manifest so that all would have to recognize it. He who had come in great humility would come again in majesty, in unmistakable glory. Much in Jesus' teaching refers to this contrast between present veiledness and future manifestation.

*   *   *

This glorious coming of Christ will be the end of history as we know it. This world will not just go on forever in the dismal ambiguity that we now know, nor will it just be snuffed out. There will be, not in a moment chosen by us, but in God's own appointed time, the end that will also be a new beginning — a goal and fulfillment for each of us and also for the whole creation, worthy of the good and faithful Creator. Such is the Christian hope. And hope is characteristic of the true church. Calvin was surely justified in saying (in his comment on 2 Peter 3:4), "Satan directly attacks the throat of the Church when he destroys faith in the return of Christ."

Christ's glorious coming will also mean judgment: "He will come again to judge the living and the dead," that is, those still alive when he comes and those who have died before that time.

Matthew 25:31-46 is often referred to as the parable of the sheep and the goats, but it is not really a parable.

The "sheep and goats" illustration is confined to one and a half verses and is simply used to suggest how unhesitatingly Christ will accomplish his judgment. The passage as a whole is a discourse on the final judgment. It is designed to bring home the truth that no one, when giving account of his or her life, will be meeting his or her Judge for the first time: Every one of us has been meeting our Judge, throughout the course of his or her life, in the flesh and blood of fellow human beings in their need and distress.

The judgment depicted in Matthew 25 is a judgment according to works, but not in any legalistic sense. The "righteous" of this passage have not deserved their acceptance on the ground of what they have done, but their works are an indication of the reality of their faith. Likewise, the failure of the others to show compassion has shown conclusively that, if they have professed any faith in Christ, it has been only counterfeit. Those who put their whole trust in Jesus Christ cannot help but make at least a beginning of openness to their fellow human beings in their distresses.

*   *   *

That the early church was convinced that in some sense the second coming of Christ was near and the interval before it short is generally agreed. But the view of many that Jesus himself and the earliest church were certain that the end would come within a few years and that nineteen centuries of subsequent history have proved them wrong is questionable. Were that view correct, there would surely be far clearer and more unequivocal traces in the later New Testament documents of the church's attempts to come to terms with the disappointment of its hope.

The early church was convinced that the death, resurrection, and ascension of Christ were history's supremely decisive events and that there could be no other events in the course of subsequent history of equal importance until the final coming of Christ. Therefore, we would argue, they saw — with true theological insight — all the rest of history as a sort of epilogue after the last chapter, as the time of God's patience that holds back the final consummation so that the gospel can be preached, heard, and believed and a human response to God's grace can be expressed. There is a real sense in which this epilogue time, this time of God's patience, is, however long it may last, essentially short.

This whole interval between Christ's ascension and his coming again stands under the sign of his command to "keep alert" (Mark 13:33; Matthew 24:42). We do not know when he will come. We must therefore always be ready. Calvin was not wrong to assert (in his comment on 1 Peter 4:7) that since Christ's ascension "there is nothing left for the faithful except to look forward to His second coming with minds alert." But to watch for his glorious coming "with minds alert" is to expect and hope for his coming with proper eagerness and urgency and therefore with active and resolute engagement in the tasks of faith, obedience, and love. Our watching will certainly include witnessing to him by word and deed and serving him tenderly as he comes to us hidden in our needy and suffering fellow human beings — his brothers and sisters.

And as we thus watch, we can desire Christ's coming with eager longing (Revelation 22:20: "Amen. Come, Lord Jesus!"), awaiting our Judge "with uplifted head" (Heidelberg Catechism, question 52), confident because he will be the same One who died and was raised from the dead for us. But we can also accept with gratitude every hour, day, and year that he does not come as so much more time for repentance and for the preaching of the gospel.

– 11 –

I Believe in the Holy Spirit

In thinking about the Creed's second article (about Jesus Christ) we have been concerned with what God has done, is doing, and will do for us objectively, externally to us. Now with the third article we will be quite specifically concerned with ourselves, or, more accurately, with what the eternal God does *in* us and *with* us. When we confess "I believe in the Holy Spirit," we are expressing our belief that God not only addresses his Word to us externally, but also himself enters into us as the Spirit, in order to enable us to hear his Word, to make us open to and free for himself. This is how faith and the community of believers come into being and are sustained.

There are several common misunderstandings with regard to the Spirit, and most of them result from a failure to take the word "Holy" in the Spirit's name seriously enough. That word should impress on us that we are concerned here with God's own Spirit, the Spirit who is himself God, one with the Father and the Son.

One misunderstanding is to think of the Spirit as an impersonal power or force (or to tend toward such a way of thinking). Some sentences in the Bible, taken in isolation from their contexts and from the rest of the scriptural witness, might suggest this sort of idea. But the witness of Scripture as a whole is clear that the Spirit we are concerned with is not something that we can control, make use of for our purposes, or exploit. Those who imagine that he is at their disposal have forgotten the "Holy," forgotten, that is, that the Spirit is God, the Lord.

Another misunderstanding is to think of the Spirit as a source of new revelation going beyond God's self-revelation in Jesus. To remember that the Spirit is holy will save us from all thought of detaching him from Jesus and from being attracted by a supposed religion of the Spirit that is not Christ-centered. It will also put us on our guard against any notion of an opposition between the Spirit and Scripture. The farewell discourses of the Fourth Gospel (John 14–16) emphasize that the Spirit's part is not to lead the church beyond Jesus into some other truth, not to speak from himself, but to take the things of Jesus and clarify them for us, and so to glorify him.

The danger that the Spirit's holiness might sometimes be forgotten in the modern charismatic movement must also be reckoned with. The New Testament certainly bears witness to the presence in the earliest church of a rich variety of spiritual gifts, including some that were exciting and spectacular. Paul could thank God that he spoke with tongues (1 Corinthians 14:18). The sincerity, courage, and devotion of charismatic churches today are not to be doubted. Nor is it to be doubted that the more traditional churches could sometimes do with more enthusiasm and excitement. But, when charismatics look down on Christians who do not speak in tongues and when the place of understanding in Christian worship is disparaged (in some church circles — and not just charismatic ones — "cerebral" has become a fashionable term of abuse), it has to be asked whether there has not been serious misunderstanding.

*   *   *

What then must we say about the work of the Holy Spirit in relation to us? It is a further miracle of divine grace and mercy that, in addition to what God has done, is doing, and will do for us in Christ, he actually enters into us, in order to open us to his Word, to himself. By giving himself to us as the Holy Spirit, God sets us free from the prison of our egotism to be free for himself and for our fellow human beings. The Holy Spirit is the Spirit of freedom (2 Corinthians 3:17: "where the Spirit of the Lord is, there is freedom"). This we must try to spell out. We may do so by means of a series of overlapping statements.

The first element of the liberation that the Spirit effects is his creation of initial faith. He it is who enables us to believe in Jesus Christ in the first instance, to come to faith in Christ. Faith is not a human possibility. Luther's Catechism states: "I believe that I cannot by my own reason or strength believe in Jesus Christ my Lord or come to Him." The Spirit frees us for faith. And yet, at the same time, the decision of faith that the Spirit works in us is most truly our own free personal decision and deed. He also sustains the faith that he has created, so that we continue believing — as he abides in us and indwells us (John 14:17; Romans 8:9, 11).

Because he creates and sustains faith, he is also "the Spirit of truth" (John 14:17; 15:26; 16:13) and of knowledge and understanding (cf. Isaiah 11:2), freeing us to accept Jesus Christ as the truth, to begin to know and understand

[56]

something of the truth that he is, and to see ourselves, our fellow human beings, and all things in its light.

By exerting his power over us, the Spirit gives us a beginning of freedom from sin's tyrannical power over us and a beginning of freedom to obey God's law (cf. Romans 8:2 and 4). To put it differently, as "the Spirit of adoption" (so the RV in Romans 8:15) he gives us the freedom to be sons and daughters of God, to know ourselves as such (verse 16), and to begin to behave as such, confidently addressing God as "Father" (verse 15b) and so seeking to please him and to avoid displeasing him.

Or we may speak of his work of "sanctification" (cf. 1 Thessalonians 4:7-8; 2 Thessalonians 2:13; 1 Peter 1:2). "Sanctification" denotes the progress in holiness of living that the Holy Spirit brings about in the believer, the movement or growth toward true obedience. We are, indeed, only beginners, but, if we are Christians at all, we are at least beginning. If we show in our lives no evidence at all of the Spirit's sanctifying work, then we are not yet Christians. That seems to be the clear meaning of Romans 8:9b: "Anyone who does not have the Spirit of Christ does not belong to him."

Sanctification includes, of course, the increase and maturing in the believer of those characteristics that Paul lists in Galatians 5:22-23a as "the fruit of the Spirit": "love, joy, peace, patience, kindness, generosity, faithfulness, gentleness, and self-control." These items overlap and are intertwined. Like the separate brush strokes of an artist, added one after another until the true likeness appears on the canvas, they set before us the wholeness of a truly Christian character.

But "love," which Paul puts first in the list, sums up the whole in itself. For the sanctifying work of the Holy

Spirit is to make us free for and open to God and our fellow human beings, so that we begin to love God with all our heart, all our soul, all our mind, and all our strength and our neighbors as ourselves (Mark 12:30-31a), and go on doing so more and more.

Yet another way in which the New Testament indicates the work of the Holy Spirit is by calling him "the Spirit of life," that is, the life-giving Spirit (so Romans 8:2: cf. verses 6, 10-11, 13b). The Nicene Creed calls the Spirit "the giver of life." Romans 1:17 promises that the righteous by faith will live — live, that is, the life with God that alone is true life, the life that the believer is to begin to enjoy here and now but will enjoy in its fullness only after this life. Through the Spirit's work this promise comes to fulfillment.

There is a close connection between this life-giving work of the Spirit and Paul's association of the Spirit with hope. In Romans 8:17-30 Paul shows that the indwelling of the Spirit, of which he has spoken earlier in the chapter, produces a life characterized by hope. In Romans 15:13 he prays that the God of hope may fill the Roman Christians "with all joy and peace in believing," so that "by the power of the Holy Spirit" they "may abound in hope."

Of all else that could be mentioned of the Spirit's work, we mention finally only that it is the Holy Spirit who enables the church to bear witness to Jesus Christ. He frees the disciples to speak boldly, with confidence, and without fear of human beings. So in Mark 13:11 Jesus says: "When they bring you to trial and hand you over, do not worry beforehand about what you are to say; but say whatever is given you at that time, for it is not you who speak, but the Holy Spirit." This does not relieve the Christian preacher from the duty of preparing with all possible diligence what is to be preached. It is, rather, a warning against succumbing to anxiety and fear of human beings when we are persecuted for Christ's sake and an assurance that, when we seek sincerely to witness to Christ, we will not simply be left to our own devices.

In Acts we see the apostles again and again bearing witness with boldness, and the conviction that the Holy Spirit is the source of their boldness is implicit everywhere in the book. In some places, as in 1:8; 4:31; 9:17, 20, and in the way the Day of Pentecost is presented as the beginning of the Christian mission, this conviction is quite explicit. It is highly significant that in 1:4 the apostles are told to wait for the gift of the Spirit. From this we may draw the conclusion that without the Holy Spirit the church is powerless to witness truly to Christ and that, in all our obvious weakness and even more whenever we begin to think that we are strong, we need to pray, certainly not as a cloak for laziness on our own part but in deep humility and earnestness, "Come, Holy Spirit!"

The Holy Catholic Church,
the Communion of Saints

Much of what needs to be said here has, in fact, already been said in connection with the earlier phrases of the Creed. The church is the congregation assembled by the Holy Spirit's work of creating and sustaining faith in Jesus Christ, the company of those who believe in the one true God and who are his people, chosen and called by him not just for their own good but for the good of all humankind. The church's source and foundation is Jesus Christ. Its life flows from his death, resurrection, and ascension. Its commission is to be his witness to every human being. Its proper order and government and its worship are determined by his reign at the right hand of the Father and by his High Priesthood. It awaits in hope his glorious coming.

The church is holy. The basic meaning of "holy" is "marked off," "separate," "withdrawn from ordinary use." In the paganism surrounding ancient Israel the designation "holy" was applied predominantly to places, objects, and human persons, and only rarely to the deity concerned. In the Old Testament, by contrast, it is used primarily of God himself, denoting his otherness and the absolute authority with which he confronts human beings; the holiness of places, objects, and persons is hardly ever thought of as mechanical and impersonal but is seen, rather, as derived from God's personal will. Applied to Israel, "holy" refers to its special relationship to God as his chosen people. Israel's holiness derives from God's gracious choice. Because God revealed himself to Israel as merciful and righteous, "holy" came to have a strongly ethical content.

As used here in the Creed, the word "holy" says a number of things about the church, and in each case we may see it as having both an indicative and an imperative force. That is, it speaks of both what the church is and what the church ought to be.

That the church is holy says something about its origin. It is not an association rooted in nature, like a family, tribe, or nation, or based on human choice, like a club. It has its origin, rather, in God's free and sovereign decision.

"Holy" is also a statement concerning the church's allegiance. The church does not belong to itself; it is not its own property. Though it is ours in the sense that God means it to be our true home, it is not ours to dispose of and to arrange according to our wishes. Its only owner is God, and we are warned against behaving as though matters stood otherwise.

"Holy" points also to the church's function, which is to bear witness in the world to God and to his grace in Jesus Christ. Where it becomes careless of this task, it is insipid, salt that has lost its savor.

And "holy" describes the church's character in Christ as the church of pardoned sinners, the undeserving object of God's grace, possessing no righteousness of its own but clothed in that righteous status before God that is God's free gift in Jesus Christ. In confessing this holiness of the church, we acknowledge that, as the object of God's grace and judgment, the church is called to strive strenuously to reflect, in all its human weakness and unworthiness, something of the character of the God to whom it belongs, to seek earnestly to become more and more in its concrete existence what it already is by God's gracious decision of justification. Insofar as the church makes a beginning, even though feeble and faltering, in obeying the imperative of its holiness, it stands out in contrast to the world. But the temptation is always present for the church to deny its holiness and allow itself to be conformed to the passing age.

*   *   *

The church is *catholic*. The word means "universal" or "general." Again, this is a matter of indicative and imperative, of what is and of what ought to be. In its unity with Christ, the church is catholic, because its Lord is the Lord and Savior of all, or to use Charles Wesley's phrase, "the general Savior of mankind." But the church is also required to strive ceaselessly for catholicity and to struggle against the continual temptation and natural tendency to fall away from it.

By using the word "catholic" here we acknowledge and claim that the particular congregation to which each of us belongs is part of the one universal church. We also acknowledge our duty to do all we can to make sure that that congregation always strives to be what we claim it is when we recite the Creed and to resist every tendency to fall away from catholicity.

The church's catholicity involves its being "always

and everywhere the same and always and everywhere recognizable in this sameness, to the preservation of which it is committed."* Catholicity is a matter both of time and of place.

Where the church's hold on its Head, Christ, who is "the same yesterday and today and forever" (Hebrews 13:8), is firm, its catholicity with regard to time is maintained. But because the church is weak and faltering, it needs to struggle constantly to maintain and to value its continuity with the church of past ages and to guard against the pride that makes us try to be independent of our fathers and mothers in the faith and to indulge in individualism and desire for the latest novelty. This does not mean that we should pursue antiquarianism or favor rigidity. The gospel itself requires the church to be always open to reformation according to the Word of God. Furthermore, since the church has to exist in history, it is bound to undergo many changes and to respond to many different circumstances and needs. But its essential sameness from generation to generation has to be maintained. This temporal aspect of catholicity also involves the recognition that the church is equally for young and old and middle-aged: For a congregation to value the young above the old or the old above the young is an abandonment of its catholicity.

Catholicity is also a matter of place, of geography. The church, insofar as it is the true church of Jesus Christ, is one and the same across all national and political frontiers, across all divisions of race, color, tribe, culture, social status, and economic condition, because its Lord is the Savior and Lord of all. This does not necessarily mean that

*Karl Barth, *Church Dogmatics* IV/1 (1956), 701.

organizational unity must be sought at all costs. But it does mean that every autonomous church or denomination is required to be constantly on its guard against the danger of compromising or abandoning its catholicity. Catholicity is abandoned, for example, when in public worship a congregation or denomination, in its right concern for the neighborhood or the nation in which it is placed, forgets its obligation to embrace all humankind in its prayer (1 Timothy 2:1) or when by pursuing its own notions without regard to the faith and practice of other churches it raises up fresh and unnecessary barriers against sister churches and fellow Christians.

*   *   *

In the phrase "the communion of saints" the word "saint" represents the same Greek and Latin words as are translated "holy" in the preceding phrase of the Creed. Here there is an ambiguity, since in the form of these words used here masculine, feminine, and neuter are indistinguishable in Greek, as are masculine and neuter in Latin. Therefore, the phrase could mean in both Greek and Latin either "the sharing in the holy things" or "the sharing by the holy persons." Perhaps the ambiguity was intentional and both meanings were intended.

In any case, both meanings make good theological sense. The members of Christ's church share the holy things, that is, all that God has done, is doing, and will do for us in Jesus Christ, all the benefits and obligations that come from God's actions. Therefore, they are bound together in fellowship with one another as holy persons, made holy by the holy things that they share. The implications of the phrase are well brought out by the fifty-fifth

[64]

question and answer of the Heidelberg Catechism: "What do you understand by the communion of saints? First, that believers, all and every one, as His members have fellowship in the Lord Christ and in all His treasures and gifts. Secondly, that each one must know that he is bound to use his gifts, readily and cheerfully, for the benefit and salvation of the other members."

Here again we both confess the reality of what we believe to be true and also acknowledge our duty to try seriously to act in accord with that truth. We have here an important imperative with regard to our public worship, namely, that we should seek to order it in such a way that every member may be able to share to the full in the holy things of Christ. That will mean, for example, guarding against all self-assertive individualism in those who lead worship and also against frequent changes in a church's liturgy or the order and shape of its public worship that make it unnecessarily difficult for the ordinary member, and still more the occasional visitor, to enter intelligently into what is being said and done.

– 13 –

The Forgiveness of Sins, the Resurrection of the Body, and the Life Everlasting

The placing of "the forgiveness of sins" here in the Creed is altogether appropriate. For the church is the company of those who know that they have been forgiven and are grateful for it. The very heart of the gospel is the good news that God has worked out for us human beings his costly and altogether sufficient forgiveness through the cross and resurrection of Jesus Christ. In doing so he has shown sin in its true colors and has revealed that all human beings are sinners. In the church, where the gospel is known, sin is most clearly manifest, and self-righteousness, though extremely common, is an alien thing. Believers should have no illusion of not needing constantly to be forgiven, constantly to repent.

In this phrase of the Creed we joyfully acknowledge God's forgiveness in Christ as the ground on which alone we are able to stand. The whole of our lives needs forgiveness, and it is from and by God's forgiveness that we live. In acknowledging that this is so, we also acknowledge that mutual forgiveness must characterize the church's fellowship and that it would be intolerable if, receiving again and again God's forgiveness of our own sins, we were unwilling to forgive our fellow Christians — and, indeed, our fellow humans in general — for wrongs done to us, and also humbly and thankfully to accept their forgiveness of us.

Since there is forgiveness of sins, there is also a future for us. What the Creed has already said about the resurrection of Christ, about his ascension, about his coming again, and about the Holy Spirit, the Giver of life, the Spirit of hope, the earnest of our inheritance, has pointed forward to what it will say in its last two phrases.

The first, "the resurrection of the body," sharply distinguishes the church's hope from the belief, common among ancient Greeks and Romans and still cherished by many today, that there is an invisible part of each person that is naturally immortal and that in its own right survives the death of the body. In contrast with this view, the Christian hope accepts that the human person is a single whole, body, mind, and soul together; that the body and the material world are not to be disparaged, since God created them (while the Greeks tended to think of the soul as a prisoner in the body longing for release); that it is right to love not just our loved ones' invisible souls, but also the familiar face and figure; that the whole human being is sinner and as a whole subject to death; and that life beyond death for us is a miracle of God's grace. The wonder of that miracle is even more strikingly suggested by the Greek and Latin versions of the Creed, which have "flesh" here, not "body," "flesh" signifying even more emphatically the weakness, helplessness, and transitoriness of humanity.

The New Testament seems to point to two stages in the future life for Christians who die before the final coming of Christ (though about this there are different opinions). First, immediately on death, a Christian is received into Christ's presence in what might be called a spiritual

[67]

state. While this state is far better than the best we experience in this present life (see, for example, Philippians 1:21, 23b), it is still incomplete (in 2 Corinthians 5:3 Paul can speak of it as nakedness). It is not yet the fullness of what God has in store for us, for which we wait till Christ's coming in glory and the end of the age. The second stage is the resurrection of the body, which in Romans 8:23 Paul calls "the redemption of our bodies".

The resurrection of the body will be the restoration of each individual in the fullness of personal life, in recognizable continuity with what we now are. How God will accomplish this we cannot explain or even dimly imagine. We must resist the temptation to think in terms of some bizarre physical or chemical wonder. And we have to trust the measureless grace, faithfulness, and power of God to fulfill his promises. Our confidence rests on the fact that God has already raised Jesus Christ from the dead and on the fact that we belong to him.

Every time that we partake of the Holy Supper we receive the pledge and foretaste of the everlasting fulfillment that the last phrase of the Creed signifies: "the life everlasting." It is to that fulfillment that the resurrection of the body is the entrance. Then God's eternal purpose for us will be fulfilled, and we shall glorify God not with the feeble, unworthy, often self-centered worship that we have offered here but with perfect worship. And we shall, we believe, enjoy God forever.

Addendum

B ut the last two phrases of the Creed signify much more than the future blessedness of believers. They signify God's renewal of his whole creation, which Christ's coming in glory will inaugurate, all to which the Bible points, when it speaks of "new heavens and a new earth in which righteousness dwells" (2 Peter 3:13). That renewal will be the perfect fulfillment, altogether worthy of the God revealed in Jesus Christ, of God's original purpose for his creation. It will mean the final and complete destruction of all injustice and lies and the end of death and suffering, and will include, we may surely trust, true fulfillment for all those millions of human beings who in the course of history have lived and died in hopeless wretchedness, counted as of no importance by fellow human beings but acknowledged as his brothers and sisters by Jesus Christ.